There's This Place I Know...

Heather Lang and H. L. Hix

There's This Place I Know...

Heather Lang and H. L. Hix

Serving House Books

There's This Place I Know...

ISBN: 978-0-9862146-9-1

Cover photograph by Kelli Russell Agodon

Serving House Books logo by Barry Lereng Wilmont

Published by Serving House Books
Copenhagen, Denmark and Florham Park, NJ
www.servinghousebooks.com

Member of The Independent Book Publishers Association

First Serving House Books Edition 2015

Table of Contents

Correspondence / 126

Works Cited / 139

About the Correspondents / 141

Introduction

We care about places. Places care for us.

This collection vividly illustrates those two truths. We started this project intent on showing one sense of those sentences, and we were shown many senses. We wanted to show that all of us share a love of place, which might therefore be a reminder of common cause in the often-fractious public dialogue about the relationship between humanity and the rest of nature. We were shown that the love of place has to do with all aspects of ourselves: our relationship with nature, certainly, but also our relationships with one another, our societal well-being, our sense of the transcendent, our self-understanding, our claims of identity, and on and on.

Through individual solicitations and through open calls, we invited people to send us "picture postcards" about places they love. We got back testaments, in image and in word, to quiet places and noisy places, solitary places and crowded places, rooms and porches, mountains and streams, and on and on. The places are various, and so is the love.

All of the responses are visible at the "Picture Postcards" blog: to view them there, go to www.hlhix.com, click on the red IN QUIRE button, and then on the "Picture Postcards" button. This book presents a selection from those postcards, and we hope you will enjoy and value them as much as we do.

Doorkijkje: See-Through Doorways

Although the see-through doorway can be observed in paintings created centuries earlier, *doorkijkje* became a prominent motif in the 17th century by Dutch artists such as Nicolaes Maes and Pieter de Hooch. This topos allowed the artist to create a more complex sense of space and to explore a deeper sense of implied narrative. Ivo Blom, exploring the trans-medial intermediality of these frames in, for example, Luchino Visconti's films, notes that "While we are inside in the world of culture, the window offers a view towards nature outside; with the door, however, we can stay within the world of culture, of domestic space."

We open the present compilation by exploring yet another medium, the picture postcard, as a frame and a passageway in and of itself, and, also, in the cases of these first entries, what Blom might describe as the "frame within the frame." This section's contributors welcome you into, and set an inquisitive tone for, this collection's examination of the ways in which postcard correspondence allows us to access other times, spaces, and events.

Dan Stockman

At Fairleigh Dickinson University, behind the gorgeous, former Vanderbilt-Twombly mansion, at the edge of the manicured gardens, is a broken gate, leading to a wild place. The shrubbery there has grown into straggly trees, the trees have grown unchecked, the grass is tall and weed-choked. And all of it is tucked away, just a few steps from where wedding parties pose for photographs, where visiting writers expound upon their craft. You just need to know to look around the corner, to take your eyes off the fountain and see what lies beyond the walls…

Gail Denham

The last two years, our vacation times have been spent searching and photographing old mining/ghost towns. A place we really enjoyed was Berlin, Nevada. This is now a State Park. The Park system has done a splendid job of preserving the past as intact as possible, labeling houses that still stand, placing placques at the site of where a home stood, and keeping the gold mine workings and buildings as they were decades ago.

One thing I love is to stop at a home site, a grave, a dilapidated house and imagine who might have lived there — how did they manage without water or electricity — what were their entertainments — where did they buy supplies? So many questions. This gate that stands in a family's back yard must have squeaked open many times as the family visited neighbors, went to a country store down the road; or to allow the family to carry the coffin of their small child to its resting place down the hill.

Berlin captures my imagination. It allows my mind to wander through "what ifs" and stories, many of which will never be fully known. It's a site worth visiting. Plan to spend several hours. Up the hill from here is an RV park, but somehow the state has managed to keep this "ghost town" in a state of perpetual historical perspective, allowing the visitors to flesh out stories for themselves, and wonder…?

J.C. Pérez-Duthie

There is no miller's daughter trying to spin straw into gold. No Rumpelstiltskin in sight. Instead, as I stroll past the crumbling shell of what was obviously once a regal hacienda, its grandeur long overrun by weeds and decay, I am surprised to find that it is not entirely abandoned. That in a nearby shed there are still men tending to the dried sisal, or the henequen fiber from the agave plant, once the "green gold," as it was called, that turned Mérida into one of Mexico's wealthiest cities. That is, until synthetic fibers came along, sending the industry and everything around it into a decline from which it has never recovered. Of the more than 1,000 haciendas that existed during its heyday, only about 400 remain standing. A few have been brought back to their former glory, if in the shape of hotels. Others have been renovated as homes, or serve as museums, paying homage to days gone by. The one I wandered through, and which sits right next to the ancient Maya ruins of Aké, however, refuses to die. As sturdy as twine.

Sophia Egbelo

Location: Obudu Mountain Resort, Cross River, Nigeria

The Obudu Mountain Resort is a vast wilderness of beauty and magnificence. My visit to this hidden sanctuary located in West Africa left me connected to the place of my ancestral roots. The untainted nature of its quiet water falls, open dirt roads and tall mountains resonates that the continent Africa still has plenty of beauty and strength yet to be told.

Randolyn Zinn

A tobacco drying barn in the fields of Fuente Vaqueros, Spain, Federico Garcia Lorca's birthplace. In town, I toured the family house museum (no photos allowed), where I saw his cradle and piano. Outside his mother's kitchen stood an old pomegranate tree that I like to think was growing there when he was a child. Upstairs, his selected drawings, poetry notebooks, and first editions were displayed in glass vitrines in the tourist center where we all sat down to watch a too-short, silent film clip of the young poet in overalls, smiling as he unloaded scenery from the back of a truck for La Barraca, his theatrical troupe that toured the white towns of Andalucia, performing Calderon's *La Vida Es Sueño*, life is a dream.

Christine Cutler

Spoleto, Italy. The world is quiet here. Everyone should experience this peace.

Transportation, Journeys, and Expeditions

"The sentence is a vessel," write Gary Young and Christopher Buckley in "Chapter One: Let the Sentence Carry You" of *One for the Money*. "The sentence offers discipline, structure and strategy while at the same time providing a creative template that accommodates the latitude of an individual imagination." There is, of course, room for more than one sentence on a postcard, and on them we sometimes write our thoughts in fragmented sentences. This concept, however, of vessels — including implied capacities or limitations — intrigues us. For example, how do we decide what to fit within the space of a postcard? How do the capabilities of our memories function? And how are our expeditions restricted by or cultivated by our modes of transportation?

Rachel Herbert

Jet, at lunch, on top of Timber Ridge one of the highest points in the Porcupine Hills West of Nanton, Alberta. This ride makes a short day trip from our ranch Trail's End. These hills have been growing cattle for our family since the range opened and we still raise our cattle the old fashioned way: free-range on grass, water, and sunshine. These hills bring us more than physical sustenance, though it is the water from the fresh cold springs in these hills that brings life to the rest of the prairies. These hills mean — fast horses, high hill tops, big sky, sweet spring water, comfort of the cabin cradled at their base, flowers, flower, flowers, I can live my history, sun, snow, secret canyon, grass, space, peace.

Beth Browne

Cedar Bush Bay, NC — Everywhere we go in Pamlico Sound looks like a postcard, but it's places like this I love the most. On the southern tip of Roanoke Island, a series of sandy spits breaks up the swell and provides habitat for red-winged blackbirds and unusual species of gulls. The water is salty. We have the warm breeze all to ourselves.

Richard Retzlaff

A great place to ponder the world's many facets both good and bad.

Julianne Couch

The Mississippi River has been in flood stage most of the summer, meaning very little pleasure boating, fishing or skiing going on here in Bellevue, Iowa. Barges still lock through Lock & Dam 12 several times a day, with locals coming out to watch. Usually the barges carry coal or grain. I couldn't see inside this one: it may have been empty.

Tim Lindner

This is Pier A in Hoboken, NJ in early fall, 2012. Across the Hudson River from Manhattan, one of the fifty-three Ginkgoes planted in remembrance of the Hoboken residents that lost their lives on September 11, 2001 eagerly reaches for autumn.

Kaitlin McClary

In my first trip to the West Coast, I have found California to be incredibly beautiful (albeit a bit chillier in May than I would have expected).

This little cove is at Point Lobos State Natural Reserve. I'd suggest going there if you've never been before. There are some lovely sights to see.

Kahle Alford

On the road.

Ireland, where I always want to be.

We rented a car, got married, found the farm and the graves and my cousin, Brendan. He still lives on the old family farm. I stood on the stone floor in the house where my great-grandmother was born. Everything was familiar and smelled of cinnamon. It's like we never left.

Connemara National Park
Co. Galway
Ireland

Naomi Ward

I was a member of the 2004 expedition that collected this deep-sea coral in the Gulf of Alaska using the submersible Alvin. Here is what I wrote about my Alvin dive: "On Wednesday, a kilometer under the surface of the sea, we glided over a Seussian landscape of pocked manganese-covered boulders on which corals and sponges had found a foothold to grow. Many of the sponges were towering white inverted cones, slender at the bottom site of attachment, and widening as they reached up into the water column. Others were squat, white, and puffy, or bright yellow and fabulously ruffled like a flamenco dancer's skirt.…We had reached a coral paradise, with delicate filigreed white primnoids, the bulbous pink paragorgias (bubblegum corals), and both branched and unbranched bamboo corals. The unbranched ones were slender pale commas, spirals, or question marks. The branched bamboos were majestic candelabras, many adorned with the sweeper tentacles at the base....Sprinkled among this framework of sponges and corals were red spider crabs, little darting shrimp with demon-red eyes that glowed in the reflected light, fat white starfish that looked like pin-cushions, orange tufted anemones, and the sinuous arms of sea stars. Often these creatures were festooned over the larger corals, perhaps using the elevation to reach a more favorable spot in the water column. The crabs were frequently seen with their claws extended out into the current, maybe waiting for a meal to float by. The dominant fish seems to be the rat-tail; we would see their long dark shapes swishing over the sea floor. One swam right under my viewport, and I could look down on its bony head and enormous dark eyes."

Sally Showalter

The countryside of San Miguel de Allende where time travels backwards and invites you to sit.

Ron Frost

Narsaq, tropical southwest Greenland. The Icebergs around Narsaq move only during the full moon so every month there is a new pattern of bergs in the bay.

Danielle Lorenz

6:09 AM, August 13, 2012. Sunrise from the High Level Bridge overlooking the North Saskatchewan River and the Alberta Legislature.

I moved to what is most-commonly known as Edmonton, Alberta, to begin my doctoral studies. Living my whole life in the traditional territories of the Haudenosaunee and Anishinaabe peoples — more specifically, Brampton, Caledon East, Hamilton, and Ottawa; all in the province of Ontario — moving to Treaty Six territory meant there was much I needed to learn.

The nêhiyaw (Cree) call the place that became Edmonton amiskwaciwâskahikan (Beaver Hills House). It is also known in nêhiyawêin as pêhonan (Meeting Place), because it is where nêhiyaw, Nakawē, Niitsítapi, Métis, and

Îyârhe Nakoda peoples would gather. One of these places happens to be where the Alberta Legislature now sits.

As the sun rose that morning, I recognized that I was about to embark on new understandings of who I was, where I came from, and what it meant to live in Edmonton — a place where the climate, geography, and histories were so much different than what I was familiar.

Just like the dawn of that new day there is so much that has yet to come to pass for me, both personally and academically. This land has many stories, and I hope to hear more of them during my time here.

Tynia Thomassie

Greetings from my fav place in the world: my meditation chair. When my arse is parked in said comfy brown, I escape my body and the material world. Here "bloated nothingness" (thanks Ralph Waldo) dissipates and I align with Divine Flow. Said chair, Yale Terrace, West Orange NJ, the most serene spot on the globe. Fav time of day/fav place: 5:30 to 6AM. (She clicks her red heels 3 times.) Tah tah!

Emilene Ostlind

Here's a snapshot of the face of the Bighorn Mountains and a bunch of — what are they, cedar waxwings? — perched in some burned pine trees. You'll see more of the burn in the background: a face of standing dead trunks on white snow contrasted to the more distant slopes the fire didn't reach. This spot is only a few miles from where I grew up and where my folks still live. I've walked past these trees probably close to a hundred times. The picture was taken from the shoulder of Red Grade Road, which is closed to cars and trucks in the winter. It's an uphill 3-mile walk to the top where there's a view into the high country, and then a fast, narrow ski run back down to the parking lot at the bottom. Red Grade and the Bighorns are where I learned to carry everything I need for a week on my back, to start a fire, to name birds and wildflowers, to carve on a snowboard, and several other of the most important skills I have. Thank heavens there's a vast alpine wilderness area in these mountains full of talus slopes and tarns and marmots or I wouldn't be the person I am today.

Boundaries, Paths (Some of Least Resistance), and Getting Lost

What if epics needed to be pared down to fit on the back of a postcard? In the introduction to his translation of *Beowulf*, Seamus Heaney writes of scholars of the past whose focus on the verse was primarily academic and how, in the 1930's, J.R.R. Tolkien published a paper in which he "assumed that the poet had felt his way through the inherited materials." Tolkien, Heaney says, "assumed, in other words, that the Beowulf poet was an imaginative writer rather than some kind of back-formation derived from nineteenth-century folklore and philology." Perhaps what we tend to share via postcards is not the events but, rather, the less tangible experience of the journey.

Dede Cummings

My father told stories all the time. He'd plan our Sunday outing and would ferry us out through the small channel going against the tide. He would talk to me mostly, as the younger girls were chatting aimlessly with Shirley in the front of the boat and the wind carried their words away with the offshore breeze. I'd constantly ask him: Who lived here? What did the Narragansetts do? What was it like in the Great Hurricane when your family lived in their summer home?

"Red, right, returning." My farmer taught me that navigation directional as he coasted around rocks and drove the boat into channels. There was one cove that had nothing but high spartina and flocks of white egrets. He'd always go in there and cut the engine. The boat would coast, and the chatter would cease. He'd raise a finger to his lips and look around, daring us to look through the tall grass, or out through the channel to the sea beyond.

That was my time with him. The other sisters and Shirley would begin to get all wound up as soon as the motor started. I kept on gazing back at the spartina, the longing so intense it felt like I was being pulled back by some unknown undertow.

Shelby Perry

I am the newest member of the BCA staff, and started my work here this summer as a wilderness inventory specialist. This means that I have had the privilege of spending the majority of my summer camping in proposed wilderness areas in and around the Red Desert in Wyoming. I wanted to share a photo from my adventures out there this summer for your postcard project. This photo was taken in the Red Creek Badlands, an area just South of Rock Springs, WY. This was my favorite (despite it also being the longest and most difficult by far) site that I visited. The area is absolutely beautiful and so rugged yet so fragile, a single vehicle trip in the light soils can collect water and erode into a massive gully. One of my goals for this site is to try to convince the BLM to limit vehicle traffic to designated routes only, so that the land will still be accessible to folks who want to enjoy it for recreational purposes without further degrading the natural beauty of the area.

Duane L. Herrmann

Magical Spot

This magical spot is part of the farm I grew up on in eastern Kansas. Going there I am renewed and encouraged because of the message it sends through the seasons. The creek is not spring fed, and has water only when we have abundant rain, this is spring and late fall into winter. The flowing water, with its music over the rocks, completes the magic. This non-permanence of the water is a lesson. Life flows. Sometimes it flows with enchantment, sometimes it flows without, but be patient: the enchantment will return.

Jean-Paul Richard

Who says you have to work hard to see beautiful scenery on foot? Strolling along the C&O Canal near Washington DC is still one of the most scenic walks in the Eastern U.S. This was a great way to celebrate my 77th birthday yesterday.

Tazio Ruffilo

Got lost in Old Orchard Beach, Maine, a couple weeks ago with my girlfriend, Amanda. We arrived as the sun was setting and a few days before the snow. Had the whole beach to ourselves until an older gentleman strolled by with his bulldog puppy. Found out he was from New Jersey too, about 10 minutes from my hometown. He told us he came to Old Orchard Beach in the 60s and has only been back to visit NJ twice. Next time someone tells you to get lost, try Old Orchard Beach.

Kevin Keen

It is quite literally an oasis in the desert. Surrounded by the Sonora Desert just outside Tucson, Arizona, Agua Caliente Park is a palm-covered, spring-fed, tranquil refuge.

Tracey Michae'l Lewis-Giggetts

I'm sitting here admiring the head rivers of the Chesapeake Bay during my visit to the Sandy Cove Retreat Center in MD and I realize not-so-suddenly that I'm at a crossroads.

Oh which way to go...

There's something about a sunset.

Perspective: Literal and Figurative

Museum of Modern Art Curator Emeritus John Elderfield asks, of Italian artist Giorgio de Chirico's Gare Montparnasse (The Melancholy of Departure), "perhaps we have to wonder whether the world depicted here is operating like a real world?" He asks because "the perspective is actually working against itself. The road, for example, on which we see the two small figures is hardly receding at all. Nonetheless, the structure to the left of that road is receding massively."

Elderfield explores this painting of the metaphysical style. According to Matthew Gale, a definitive quality of metaphysical art is "fictive space [which] was created in the painting, modeled on illusionistic one-point perspective but deliberately subverted." He continues, "Within these spaces classical statues and, most typically, metaphysical mannequins (derived from tailors' dummies) provided a featureless and expressionless, surrogate human presence."

While the picture postcards in this collection are largely photographs, it is intriguing to ponder the viewpoints, such as low, high, and aerial, among others. And then, of course, there is the point of view of the writer, as well. The similarities and the differences captivate us. We consider what type of human presence is offered by the visual aspects of the postcards, and what is brought to the correspondence only by the piece's written content.

Renée K. Nicholson

I am telling you this story because you are the only person who will not judge me.

And you didn't get all that mad when I borrowed your silk blouse without telling you and spilled cheap cabernet down the front of it in a long, grape-y smudge that the cleaners couldn't get out.

Do you remember that?

You were still with Tyler then—oh Tyler—and you could never really be with a Tyler because of the shaggy bangs, dirty blonde and keg-o-rators and cars with iffy transmissions, floorboards mashed with remnants of Taco Bell.

I remember that blouse, smooth between the fingers and robin's egg blue, draped across my torso like a slick, bright waterfall.

It happened when I went to meet Brett, who had a few pictures in that show, black and white photographs —

Remember how we thought black and white was the height of sophistication, like filet mignon and restaurants that park your car for you, where the cheapest bottle of wine is over fifty bucks and we'd pretend not to care. That wine of our youth, fermented in memory, all the bottles and glasses and stained clothes and the all those things we wished with each satisfying pop of the cork.

Choa Choi

Helena, Montana, U.S.A.

This photo is taken from a house through the big glass window, facing Mt. Helena. I found my summer in Montana the most embracing yet menacing days of my life. During my stay in Montana, I regularly prayed Thee to procure some herbs that will make me fall into hazy oblivion. Some words, thick jazz drumming my soul, and sweat-churning labor were in need. To go on living in feigned indifference with the incurable disease or to pursue the daunting spirit gorged with youthful verve was the question at stake.

William D. Hicks

From the lakefront to the downtown shopping and restaurants there is much to see and do in Saugatuck Michigan. There are also the farms and sunrises that can't be beat. And being that it's only a couple hours away from Chicago, it's the perfect getaway from big city life.

Elizabeth Boleman-Herring

Late October. It is my favorite season. The tourists have finally conceded that their thin summer cottons are no defense at all against the chill of a Mediterranean autumn. They have all, all gone home now, far to the north and west, to don their coats and hats. Just before dawn, I am alone atop the cliffside hamlet of Imerovigli. In the dark, I knew it was one of those unique mornings on the caldera, that immense blasted bowl of water, lined by the flimsy cliffs that are Santorini: the island is nothing if not negative space. Once upon a time, the earth expanded her ample cheeks, like Dizzy Gillespie, and blew 40 cubic kilometers of matter into the air, leaving only the tiny crust of ground upon which I clamber today. At first, there is nothing at all but fog. White, white mist through which I cannot make out white, white buildings. A dead pit viper lies at my sandaled feet, the victim of some wily cat of the Greek night. I look up from its still form and the fog thins. Like cream, whipped to impossible fineness, it sloshes in the bowl of the caldera. Up and down, up and down, in the silent dawn wind. It comes pouring over the cliffs from the warmer, sunnier, dawn-side of the island, streaming down the sheer, dark stone faces to the sea. I stand at the apex of the event, the fog parting around me. I will never see this again. I will never be just here again.

Kelli Russell Agodon

On the warmest and sometimes the coolest summer days, we jump from this dock into Puget Sound. We are everyone: men, women, mothers, fathers, kids, teenagers, grandparents, hippies, yuppies, travelers, introverts, extroverts, and those who have avoided any labels. When we leap, we are an open-ended question about diving in. And every time, we trust our bodies will save us.

There is usually a cloud somewhere, but there is also blue sky. Like life, it always depends where you look.

Jeff Bloedel

Pike's Peak. I hiked from Manitou Springs up to the peak with some friends in 2009. This was a journey of self-discovery. At the time, our family was on the brink of collapse. My wife was in the hospital and there seemed no hope for us at all. I hiked up on a whim and didn't think I could do it. I told myself the whole way up that there was no way I was going to be able to summit. How did I make it? One foot in front of the other. As I looked out at the amazing vistas I realized something, our family might not make it, but as long as we're putting one foot in front of the other, that's really all that matters. Right after I took this picture I broke down. I wept and my group of friends held me until I finally was empty. I was empty of fear, anxiety, and loneliness. I felt strong and hopeful for the first time in a long time. Every time I see this picture I am instantly transported back to this time and am able to tell myself, "One foot in front of the other."

Melissa Esposito

This is where I feel most at home. I wish everyone could feel so free.

Alanna Coogan

Not with a Fizzle, but with a BANG: How Easter is Celebrated in Florence, Italy

Stefan Strychar

This is a picture of my favorite spot back home - the oft-abandoned, pseudo-renovated, eyesore/heart-warmer Michigan Central Station in Detroit. Photographed ad nauseum over the last few years as a symbol of blight and decay, it reminds me of more prosperous days decades ago, and driving past it on a daily basis, dropping my father off at work downtown. Every time I go home, I drive past it and get another angle.

So many photographers take the iconic and familiar shots from the front... but no one ever takes the time, care, or love to get a picture from behind... so here it is.

Cory Johnston

When we emerged from dinner at The Porterhouse that night, Dublin's Temple Bar district had been transformed into its own tiny, independent city. Everywhere, there were people. They drank, ate, juggled fire, played guitar. And although this district only spans a handful of city blocks, and my trip lasted but one week, my memory prefers this picture: how the fading sky stretches down the pedestrian zone towards infinity; how the colors melt, merge, flare; the way the bustling motion of this space is rendered still, yet retains its own palpable vitality, as though these people might suddenly burst back to life, if only I could better recall what happened next.

C. Lee Faris

I held you on my lap as we gazed into the space where horizon and ocean melded into one long, unreachable rope. You were five, and I felt infinite.

Diegesis

As far back as Plato's *Republic*, we've been contemplating the concepts of *diegesis*, or telling, and *mimesis*, or showing. What can an image tell us? Often writers are instructed to, figuratively, show not tell, but when it comes to commercial postcards, it is typically the telling – the literal writing on the postcard – that personalizes the correspondence. Ultimately, the two work together to share an experience either through supplementation, juxtaposition, or sometimes both.

Bill Reiners

During the early years of my career as an ecologist, I was on the Dartmouth faculty and much of my research was done in New Hampshire's White Mountains, particularly on Mt. Moosilauke, an outlying mountain that was the property of the college. The peak itself was windswept alpine tundra surrounded downslope by dense thickets of balsam fir krummholz. But in the Mt. Blue saddle about 1000 m to the north was a flat, protected spot where the fir trees grew tall for this elevation (ca 4,000 ft). This was a hiker's refuge from the wind and featured a relatively open forest interior over a dense, fern ground cover. According to a college legend, Mt. Moosilauke was inhabited by an immortal, Faustian character named "Doc Benton" who roamed the mountain through the centuries, spying, thieving, and doing perhaps worse things to campers who dared to stay on the upper flanks of the mountain. I knew from the mystical, cloud-swept, fog-dripping, lichen-encrusted character of this place, that it had to be one of Doc Benton's primary abodes. As we did our research there, I occasionally looked over my shoulder, knowing he watched us as we worked in this special place. We never stayed overnight in Doc's domicile.

Suzanne Richter

A POTENT REPELLENT.

The south has many fascinating traditions. Last summer I watched a young mother, new to our neighborhood, labor day after day to paint the ceiling of her porch a beautiful light blue. The baby fussed and cried in the bouncer. Her progress was slow but steady.

The blue color is used to ward off "haints," restless spirits of the dead who have not yet moved on from the physical world. The color confuses the ghosts into believing the ceiling is a river or other body of water which they cannot cross. After the young mother was all done painting the ceiling, she hung up these three blue bottles to act as evil spirit catchers.

Enslaved African-Americans brought this tradition with them from Africa. Southerners (of all ethnicities) continue to paint their porches and make "bottle spells" because "that's what their grandmothers did and their grandmothers before them."

Letisia Cruz

Maybe you will like this picture. It was taken down in Key West about two years ago. The square was crowded, as it is most sunsets. Kids were running around, cats, roosters, a few jugglers and some boys playing with fire. I leaned over the fence to try and get a shot of the sunset and this guy and his dog just floated into view. (That's his dog there in the front of the canoe — hard to see because my camera sucks.) I remember thinking they had the right idea.

Brian Bradford

Love a urinal you can hide in. Men's room at PJ Clarke's. Corner of 55th and 3rd NYC.   Bumped into Mickey Rourke here one afternoon, years ago. Had a brief but interesting discussion about Charles Bukowski. And if that ain't enough, Johnny Mercer penned what is arguably the greatest saloon song (One for my Baby made famous by Sinatra) ever on a bar napkin here. The bartender that night was a fella named Tommy Joyce. Urban myth has it that Mercer ("So set 'em up Joe. Got a little story you ought to know") apologized profusely to Joyce because he could not come up with a decent rhyme for "Tommy." Great bacon-cheeseburgers. Best seat in the house—back room by the clock.

Documenting Change and Loss

While analyzing a painting by Italian Artist Paola Tavoletti, poet, illustrator, and editor Letisia Cruz contemplates loss, writing that "shared grief is, if only slightly, a lesser burden. Sometimes simply knowing that someone was here before is enough to inspire us." We can pause briefly, "knowing that someone else has experienced the weight of our burden. Suddenly, though perhaps only momentarily, we see beauty once more." And, so, sometimes in times of change and loss, we reach out to one another.

Amy Hartley

This piece of bone sits alone, with no trace of the skeleton it once was a part of. A massive pelvis, lacking a spine, I can think of no animal in Alaska's interior large enough to warrant it. The bone is situated ornamentally near a walking path at a park in Fairbanks. Just how old is this decaying cairn? How far has it come? Any connection to its past has crumbled away, like the fine powder that rolls beneath my palm when I run my hand down the flank of the misplaced behemoth. No longer part of the scaffolding beneath muscle and hide, it's now home to who knows how many shrews, insects, and soon, wild raspberries. This puzzling find is a reminder that the process of wane and rot is also a blossom of reinvention.

Michele Leavitt / Stephen Mulkey

The Ichetucknee River in North Florida. A rainy winter and spring has allowed the water levels to rise, flooding the cypress swamps and deepening the channel. The rains opened the way for this manatee, the first we've ever seen in this river.

Brenda Saunders

Greetings from Windora!

I 'm on a Birding Trip to the Channel Country in Western Queensland. This lovely bird is an Apostle bird so called because it lives and travels in a family group of ten to twelve. His plumage blends in well with the Mulga trees in the area. The long drought has brought them in close to townships and tourist sites looking for hand-outs (and they do feed from your hand). Sadly they' re now seen as a pest. Safety in numbers is their motto!

Regards
Brenda

Josh A. Weinstein

Greetings from Wagadake! I hope you are well, and enjoying the turn toward summer. This photo is from this time of year, but taken several years ago. Nevertheless, it brings me back each time—to the green mountains of northern Honshu, and the natural hot springs that dot the area. This ridge, part of the Ou Range, separates Iwate and Akita prefectures, and on a day like this one it's truly breathtaking. After driving past working farms, a small abandoned clear-cut logging operation, and several rusted vehicle chassis to arrive at the trailhead, the hike nearly straight up through a shady cedar forest, giving way to an ancient, nationally protected old-growth beech forest is unforgettable, and wordlessly conveys what is at stake in restraining high-impact human activities.

With Blessings,
Josh

Arwen Fleming

My partner and I spent a week last April at a cottage north of Bracebridge, Ontario. I took this photograph at the edge of a river, just downstream from a small waterfall. The foam builds up at the base of the waterfall, and you can see insects playing above the foam just at the river's edge. (Luckily for us, there were no mosquitos yet.) We were there in time for the very first signs of spring, when the earth begins to thaw out and smell like dirt again. Small shoots were growing, and a few very tiny mushrooms.

Today I find myself longing for spring in Montréal, where a 4-foot pile of snow is growing at the side of my front porch.

Erik Molvar

Adobe Town is one of the West's most spectacular and outstanding crown jewel landscapes, where thick beds of volcanic ash have been sculpted into fragile pinnacles, arches, and palisades. It is the largest and most spectacular of Wyoming's desert wilderness candidates, and is currently at risk from oil and gas drilling that is encroaching from the east.

Renée E. D'Aoust

We call this our little long dog fall hike of 2013. We climbed from 4300 feet to 8000 feet. Tootsie, our mini dachshund, doesn't ever seem to feel the elevation change, but I sure do! We're on top of Mannlibode, in Valais, and those are the Swiss Alps in the distance. Sometimes I think Switzerland is one big hill.

Ed Sherline

I'm writing to you from the Laramie town dump. It is one of my favorite places to take a half an hour break to look around. I'll find any excuse to go here: today it was an old kickstand that needed to go in the scrap metal heap. Even the locals don't realize that the dump has some of the best views in the area, sitting up on a flat plain and away from houses. There's always something new to see here. It is a constantly changing place. This postcard is of Mount Woodchip, with its precipitous east face. By the time I find the nerve for a summit attempt, it will probably have been carted away for landscaping.

Light and Geometry

Having contemplated loss and change, how do we move forward? Patterns in history suggest that we should look ahead by studying the past, so, as a complement to the previous section of postcards, we were reminded of the *Yi Jing* (Changes), an ancient Chinese divination manual based upon sixty-four hexagrams balancing heaven (yang) and earth (Yin), a balance that reflects what Conrad Schirokauer and Miranda Brown call "the conviction that nature and man are interrelated." On the impact of Han philosophy, Schirokauer and Brown write, "The acceptance of the idea that all phenomena are interrelated in a set of correspondences gave great satisfaction. Not only did it explain everything, but it enabled humans to feel at home in the world, part of a temporal as well as a spatial continuum." We find something of that hope and balance in the postcards that imbue this section with light and geometry.

Edith "Ish" Bicknell

View of Penobscot Bay from Little Deer Isle, Maine

When I gazed out on this scene, my heart thumped and my mind wailed. I couldn't stop snapping pictures as the clouds evolved into this monstrous presence. Wish you were here.

Charity Kittler

I love wandering through cities on foot, camera in hand. And what better city to explore — what better neighborhood— than my own? This was taken in Uptown (north side of Chicago) at night. And it reminds me of Uptown — a little off kilter, a little hard to understand at first, known for bright lights and shadier areas. Haha. Home sweet home.

Rupert Loydell

This is the view from Enzo's in Tuscany, where we go each summer, as night arrives. After a day out exploring the countryside, eating well, looking at art, and at least one swim in the pool, we sip local wine and watch the light fade. We are warm through, and truly relaxed; we are counting down the days until this year's visit — our eighth or ninth.

Paula Wright

Thanks for your note; I hope you're well! It has been a month since I moved from Wyoming to Eugene, Oregon, where I sit writing to you. A bit overwhelmed by the experience of driving through the big city and the experience of bicycling in traffic (!), I found the Ridgeline trail system a welcome haven. I took the photo below with my phone as I was hiking up Mt. Baldy (at the grand elevation of 1,232 ft). After a steady diet of brown grass and blue sky in WY, the green of this place overwhelmed me! The first part of the hike takes you through an enchanted forest — moss and lichens bursting from every crevice in the trees and ivy coating the ground. Rising above the Willamette River, the trail takes you to a small prairie up at the summit. There, with the yellowing grasses and with the Cascade Mountains in view to the East, it felt a bit like back home.

Carol Fragale Brill

Sitting on Cape May's Cove Beach watching the sunset over Cape May Point — Priceless.
Grateful I'm here.

Jenna Tripke

Many years ago, I made my way from the cacophony of music and chaos on the streets of Philadelphia's annual July 4th Celebration to the roof of a high-rise apartment building overlooking the Parkway. A handful of us were up there, drinking cheap beer and waiting for the grand finale fireworks show above the Art Museum that was to signify the end of the night's festivities. As I sat on the edge of the concrete rooftop, legs dangling down, I took out my phone – which housed, at the time, an unimpressive 1.5 megapixel camera — and snapped a photo of the view. Somehow, my little lens managed to catch a beautiful moment: the waiting crowds; the Art Museum, ready to bask in its moment of brilliance; the lights of the Cirra Center; the reflection of the Schuylkill River. It's not a perfect photo, but it remains one of my favorites because it captures a moment of anticipation – a moment of nocturnal quiet before the deafening whistles and explosions of light that accompany a city in celebration. It's my city, and it's quite a view.

Leah Schultz

Greetings from Rock Lake in lovely Lake Mills, Wisconsin. My parents grew up and were high school sweethearts in this lovely town, so you might say my fondness for Lake Mills is in my blood. I swam away entire summers in this lake and my dad has had a sail boat on its waters since I can remember. Pictured here is my family's pier on this small body of water that holds so many of my favorite memories.

April Heaney

We adopted our youngest son from Ethiopia six months ago, and we traveled to the capital, Addis Ababa, a couple times in the process. We couldn't believe the scaffolding that workers use in constructing new buildings; they balance on Eucalyptus poles, risking their lives every moment of the project — although the sight of the scaffolds is beautiful, too. This photo is a reminder for us of the resilience of the Ethiopian people, their simple ingenuity in the face of terrible economic times. It was an unforgettable opportunity to get to know this ancient culture.

Jeff Knops

This view from the Chihuly Garden and Glass exhibit makes the Seattle Space Needle look like it is bursting into flames or jettisoning into the stratosphere. This is the place people need to go when they are in love.

Homecoming and "Home"

The speaker in Katherine Larson's "The Oranges In Uganda" claims to "know why / people make love when they / come home from a funeral."

In an exchange about the concept of home, our friend and postcard contributor Letisia Cruz sent words that offer eloquent introduction to this section.

> I've lived in Miami for 21, going on 22 years. When I first moved here I thought it was a good place to live because even if you end up homeless, you can't die of cold in Miami.

> When I first moved to the US from Cuba, I lived in a green apartment building in Union City, NJ. To this day, I am an apartment dweller at heart. Houses have too much space. In fact, I spent a good chunk of my life living in spaces that were small enough that I could see the entire span of the place without leaving my bed — having separate rooms has been an adjustment.

> How I feel about space is relative to how I feel about the body. The vehicle is essential, but it's only a vessel.

> I counted once, and I think I've moved nearly 30 times in 39 years. I feel a sense of gratitude toward every space I've ever called home. But I never feel attached. I don't like ownership. It entails responsibility. And one thing I've learned about myself is I value freedom above all else.

> Everything is transient. One day I will leave this home. Just like one day I will leave this body. The things that make us feel "at home" also divert our attention from the fact that "home" is an illusion. It does little more than define where we are at any given moment in time.

Brenda Kay Ledford

This old barn stands on the outskirts of the mountain town of Hayesville, the seat of Clay County, North Carolina. The Statue of Liberty and an old tractor grace the front of this historical building. Freedom and heritage are the themes captured in the photo. Our little mountain town attempts to preserve Appalachian culture and the freedom many soldiers have fought for our nation and county. Strong-spirited mountain men and women know hard work and appreciate the liberty we enjoy today in America. Clay County may be the smallest county in North Carolina, but we have a heart of gold and demonstrate that by helping our neighbors who have needs.

Tom Sterner

Dusky jewels, myriad lakes nestled in the Rocky Mountains just west of Denver. Five generations of my family have fished, camped, and ridden inner tubes and rafts down the veins feeding them. This photo was snapped at Wonderland Lake at dusk in Boulder, Colorado.

Fran Hill

My favorite room in the house isn't a room at all. It's this little porch. Here, steam rises from morning coffee, bird song is heard, clouds are watched, thoughts gathered, and Scrabble games played. I love this place and think you would, too.

Anna Sangrey

Sometimes a Pirates game in Pittsburgh, Pennsylvania, waits to begin as a rainbow arcs over PNC Park. At the game this spring, I learned about baseball — I learned about being an American.

Annie Guzzo

Here I am in Paris, 10th Arrondissement in Cyril's apartment - great view of the rooftops and the Eiffel Tower. No matter how many times I see it at night, I run to the window at the top of the hour to see the sparkling lights, over and over again.. I feel like a kid at fireworks. Funny how I love Paris almost as much as I love the wide-open spaces of Wyoming. There is a bakery across the street that sells a magical raspberry rose macaron — when you bite into it you hear the angels singing. It would be fun to be in Paris together. I'd share musical history in that amazing city, and you'd tell me about poets and writers. And we'd eat too much, of course.

John Manuel

Since I was a young boy, I have hiked through Stebbins Gulch in Northeast Ohio with my friends Peter and Josh. The clear water hissing over shale ledges, the cool moist air, and the infinite shades of green of the trees and ferns always amazes and humbles me. I moved away from Ohio in my twenties, but come back every few years to visit my friends. Now in our sixties, Peter, Josh, and I have followed different paths in life. We can find it difficult initially to reconnect, but when we return to Stebbins Gulch, our differences fall away. We find ourselves immersed in timeless beauty and filled with a sense of hope and awe.

Barbara Harroun

In McNabb, IL about a half mile from the Quaker Meeting House, you'll find this massive White Oak, one of the largest in the state of Illinois. I walk to this tree every chance I get, although I live many miles away, so it tends to be about twice a year. It reminds me of the life I want to live—expansive, many branched, and deeply rooted. The glorious sight of it humbles and quiets me. The owner, a truly wonderful gentleman by the name of Dick, allows us to walk right up, sit on the lowest branch, and pet the miniature pony that often grazes in the wide circumference of its shade. Two years ago I pressed my face into its bark for the first time, listening, straining to see how far I could reach around the 23' base. The tree gives me perspective, and makes me feel small in the best way. The sight of it allows another part of me to soar, such a wonder it is to me, such a powerful reminder to keep growing.

Alex Borgen

After living in various places saturated with nature (either in direct footings or nearby locations), I have moved to Chicago for my MFA graduate studies, and the city surrounds me, encroaches my peace, collapses on my being. The buildings here are enormous, casting dark shadows in rough angles. Here, there is no starry sky to speak of; occasionally I see venus, the moon. I have found, however, by means of artistic endeavors, that Lake Michigan has been my constant salvation. Its expanse of celeste transitioning perfectly into the horizon and atmosphere above takes me with it. When looking out, I see no city, just a watery expanse. Now, I see the lake everywhere, reflected in the clouds, mirrored in the large windows of the skyscrapers, in the trembling shadows daily, and in the rainy surges of run-off in the streets. The water is my nature, salvation, my home.

Christina Ingoglia

Greetings from MO! I thought you might like to see the sweet fire pit Dave built for me for our wedding. I've been taking full advantage of it — having friends over to make s'mores, enjoying fall nights fireside, contemplating life, liberty, and the moon, etc. I seem to come up with more and more excuses to sit outside and by that fire. Wish you were here. Hope all is well!

Daniella Bondar

My first weekend living alone in Manhattan, I stumbled upon the red doors. It was hard to tell what I was looking at, until I was greeted by a neon Budweiser sign. I pictured groups of burly men sitting inside with pitchers watching something sports related. The glow of twinkle lights from inside danced along the windows. I pulled the heavy door open and tiptoed inside. They filmed some *Godfather II* here. The lanky man was talking to me but staring at the bartender. His Ramones t-shirt had a grape-sized hole in the back. I nodded and lifted my beer towards him. Knowing this little fact made me feel connected to the city. I knew one of those things that real New Yorkers know. I keep going back, always taking a wooden table in the back. The broken booths and dirty bathrooms comfort me when I need them too. There's a pink neon sign in the back that reads Prostitution.

Lori Berezovsky

Here is the front yard of the home I grew up in (DeKalb, IL), and where my 88-year-old mother still lives. I spent many happy hours under the big Norway Maple playing Barbies, and I spent many more happy hours climbing the same tree. Mom gets older but somehow the yard remains impossibly the same. When I go home, I let that little girl inside of me come out and play.

Pamela Banting

I am sending you this photograph of the natural grass prairie on Providence Ranche, a few kilometres west of my house near Calgary. I took the photo one day in June when the owner, Hamish, his partner Rita and his son Dylan took us on a walk on one part of the ranche. It was a glowery day and the likelihood was that we would get drenched at any moment, though we never did. The photo shows the Wildcat Hills, which are the hills I can see right this minute from my study window, and in the foreground there are a few spent dandelions, a yarrow plant about to bloom, the toothed leaves of either a windflower or a Canada anemone, and, best of all, the magenta flowers of three-flowered avens, a.k.a. prairie smoke, a.k.a. Old Man's whiskers, one of my favourite plants. I have two of them in my front yard I love them so, and I wish there were more of those sprightly elfin presences.

The land that is the Providence Ranche has been in Hamish's family for several generations, and he is very knowledgeable about the ranch history of the area near the town of Cochrane and very proud of his stewardship of the land. Hamish's ancestor, who for a time managed the historical Cochrane Ranche for whom the town is named, actually has a cameo in my husband's penultimate novel, Lightning, a literary western set mostly in Montana and also in Alberta.

I myself was born and raised in the boreal forest in central northwestern Manitoba: I grew up in the bush. One of the ways I connect with the place I now live in the foothills of the Rockies is through my lifelong affection for wildflowers. I learned the names of the flora of this area by taking pictures of each kind of plant and making my own album / 'field guide'. I am tied to this land now by virtue of its muscular and sensuous beauty, by its flora and fauna, and by the novels and anecdotes of lifelong Albertan and novelist Fred Stenson. If there is reincarnation, I want to come back as a wildflower and stay outside in all kinds of weather and never miss a thing.

Juxtaposition: Unusual Neighbors

In this project, we were inspired by the collaborative efforts of the French surrealists, their strong sense of the image, and their tendencies to juxtapose. We were also encouraged by Peter Schulman and Josh A. Weinstein's *Green Humanities*, which envisions "varied collaborations and juxtapositions of scholarship within the humanities as well as environmental sciences and related fields." Not unlike the mission of Schulman and Weinstein's journal of ecological thought in literature, philosophy, and the arts, we found ourselves among picture postcards that work toward finding common ground for dialogue in a love of places.

Linda Aleta Tame

I snapped this photo in the Orthodox district of Jerusalem in 2006. Through the drizzling rain on the bus window I saw a flash of yellow, a little girl's umbrella contrasting the dogmatic statement of a man in black. It afforded relief from the pervasive gray scale. But for that bit of sunshine and a few punctuations of pink, purple, and blue, the scene would have seemed void of promise. And that's where I saw myself then, somewhere between the black and yellow.

Rick Hasenauer and Patricia A. Nugent

Arrived late this afternoon, in time to enjoy the sunset at our Adirondack paradise. Our 'neighbors', the ducks along shore and the eagles farther up our side of the mountain, were part of the welcoming committee. Big decision ahead: Which chair on the dock to relax in tomorrow?! Hope you join us here soon. (We'll invite the 'neighbors' when you do!)

Di Brandt

A snippet of my garden in early fall, in that tender moment when some of the leaves are already brown and shrivelled, some still bright green, and the rest just turning colour.....The twins are guardian spirits of the garden, and of our family as well.....Our family has many twins in it, I'm a twin myself and I recently become the proud grandmother of twins, Sofia and Francesca......

Renée Ashley

When I was very young my great aunt lived in a small apartment across the street from the Palace of Fine Arts in San Francisco. The Palace stood just the other side of what I thought of as the duck pond. It must have been the mid-to-late 50's, because Tante died in 1971. I remember little other than that the sun was out, the grass was really green and soft, and the ducks — wholly white ducks and the mismatched mallard pairs — were paddling around in the still water in the foreground of the Palace. I was probably only there for a half-hour or less, but it still feels like a place of cease-fire. I don't plan to ever return. It's my available peace.

James Penha

Hot and cold in the caldera atop Mount Bromo in Java. This is my kind of equinox: a place where opposites co-exist.

Emily Strauss

I love it when I can wake up early enough in a place where the sunrise will play tricks in the sky. This is the far eastern desert of Nevada looking out from Wheeler Peak down to the basin below. No one else was awake and I walked around camp, surprising a turkey and four deer by the stream. It was still cool out, and the stream made noise as it fell down the canyon. The desert is not always hot and dry, which I like to remind myself occasionally.

David Freitag

The Golden Gate Bridge and San Francisco, California. I love the meeting of city, land, ocean, and an engineering marvel connecting them all. In one place I can connect with nature and also marvel at the scale of human achievement in front of me. This spot is a favorite of mine for sitting, watching the world, and thinking about my place in it.

Jeff Lockwood

I'm having a blast in the Red Desert! I really need to come to this place more often. The land here is so empty and humbling (even a bit scary) — and it's also so at risk from the goddamn energy industry's insatiable desire to extract gas. The variety of species and habitats is incredible — from ponds to dunes to sagebrush to the iconic Boar's Tusk (upper right of the postcard). Next time I come out, you have to join me. The RD should be nearly as inspirational for a poet as it is for an entomologist — and you can't say that about many places, eh? Say "hi" to Kate for me (she can come along too, of course).

Bernard Quetchenbach

This is Steamboat Point, Yellowstone Lake, in late May, with the ice mostly gone — some years there's still ice until mid-June. It's a fire-and-ice kind of place. There are usually a few buffalo grazing across the road from the lake, and often scaup or goldeneyes out on the water. Once we watched several coyotes crossing the ice from a picnic spot not too far from here. I come from the Great Lakes, so I like having a big body of water somewhere in the general area. At Yellowstone Lake, you can see the other side, but there's a lot of water out there.

Tendai R. Mwanaka

Hemel en Aarde valley

It's a picture of the valley of Hemel en Aarde (heaven and earth valley), in Volmoed, the Western Cape, South Africa, March 2012. I took the picture on top of the surrounding mountains. Hemel en Aarde is where heaven and earth meets. When inside this valley you are surrounded by the mountains so you don't see the outside, only the earth and the skies (heaven). When heaven and earth meets it is heavenly, the place is heavenly. It is a spiritual centre. People come from all over the world to this place for spiritual regeneration, to deal with issues, to find themselves, to heal. It's when we can connect with life on earth and life in heaven when we can really connect to our truer selves.

Correspondence

In *One for the Money: The Sentence as a Poetic Form*, Gary Young and Christopher Buckley explore the concept of *Multum in Parvo*, much in little. They write that such short forms as the aphorism and epigram are "like icebergs: their bulk is below the surface, and the weight of their utterance is drawn by implication." These final postcards, short correspondence about correspondence, have, we think, that characteristic of much in little, and we leave you to experience by implication their weight.

Suzanne Roberts

Dearest,

I love this place because of its vastness, because here is the collision of nature and art. Here, you can be whoever you really are. Without the usual borders, gravity pulls from us even our names. With love and dust from Black Rock City, Sassy.

Anna Lena Phillips Bell

Not long ago I found a stack of greeting cards on a table, one of several that stand in the main post office in Durham, North Carolina. Each table is made of green glass, sturdy and scratched, and is fitted with two brass lamps like the one shown here. I love these lamps, which are so friendly and yet so elegant, and I love the tables, which are at such a height that I can rest my elbows on them, look out at the banks of post-office boxes, and commence with whatever business I have. The greeting cards were nothing special—mass-produced, with bland watercolors of flowers on them in several patterns—but they were there.

It's easy to not write a letter, even when the cards are left out for you, just by their presence making news for you to write about. Even when the lamp beckons, as if it's saying to anyone, You, too, might stand and write here, turning your head, shifting from one foot to the other; carefully address the envelope, checking each numeral; affix a stamp and walk toward the counter; drop the new letter into the brass mail slot, hearing it flap back on its hinge; and go out the revolving wooden door, feeling virtuous and satisfied, feeling the slow travel of the letter—quick, actually, so quickly it will reach your loved one—through the workings of the postal system, living in the mystery and anticipation of news not yet delivered but on its way.

On my desk at home I have put a note for myself: ALWAYS WRITE BACK. I haven't written back always, which is the reason for the note, and which is one of many reasons for the affection I feel for the post office: its very architecture supports me in the effort. These tables are not going anywhere—they're bolted to the floor. These lamps are, to borrow a phrase from Mary Wells, sticking to the table like a stamp to a letter. And each one's little halo of light waits for me to slide a card or sheet of notepaper into its circle, take out my pen, and begin.

John C. Mannone

"breeding lilacs out of the dead land"
　　　After T. S. Eliot
　　　On the Cosby Nature Trail in the Great Smoky Mountains, TN

The rhododendron spices the damp air and mist rises above the brown leaves that have fallen on the black sod. I hear their whispers as if a moist breath through feather moss. I see the dappling through the sycamores & basswoods giving resurrection to the shade. They join in harmony, with the sound of moss covering the rocks, keeping the secret of their age.

Water showers punctuate the stillness with gurgles and drips. The inexorable cycle of water: the taking of atoms of stone and rebuilding earth downstream. Only fingerprints ripple water. Rocks have long since cried out, before man. Who am I to tread on their souls, on the heart of earth, on the breath of God? How can I even listen without contaminating the air?

The river cascades, frothy bubbles swirl in the eddies and mix my memories lost in time. It was just the two of us then on this sacred ground. I crush dry leaves between my fingers, this sweet earth that I once came from and to which someday I must return. Will I leave such fragrance when I am gone?

A cool breeze shakes the trees, frees their prayers. They float to me as rainbows. I hear their quaking and the sound of many waters. And I am baptized in that sound. I die for a moment before I am reborn. I hear their spangled words, their tune rising above the stream. Every stream has its own dialect. Yet, I understand them all. She is calling me back, back to her bosom.

I am still haunted by waters. The water speaks with the same sparkle of the sun, its spray, spiked with light. Even the leaves call out my name. And a rhododendron leaf, as if I could see inside its heart, tightens like a scroll. I wonder, Is my name written there?

Jan Conn

I've been informally documenting Latin American street art for several years and this is one from Bogotá, Colombia, taken in November 2012. It is (or was) near the entrance to the Museo de Arte Moderno de Bogotá. I arrived near noon, so the door and his suit were almost fathomlessly black. He might be a politician, but his relatively relaxed body language and face suggest to me someone more like an artist, perhaps a writer.

Heather Lang

WINTER
I will stuff a small rag of
its sky into my pocket forever.
—Larry Levis

I hope this correspondence finds you well. Perhaps you've enjoyed Levis' couplet before. I discovered these lines within the pages of *One for the Money: The Sentence as a Poetic Form* by Gary Young and Christopher Buckley published by Lynx House Press, Spokane Washington, 2012. Per the permissions in the book, "Winter" was swept into our palms from an unpublished manuscript.

No, Harvey, I haven't lost my mind. Neither have you. This spring photograph, merely days old, is a snapshot of my rural Wisconsin commute. Today snow might fall only two hours north of my home; despite springtime, Wisconsin winter is never far from our minds. Perhaps, however, this is part of the pleasure.

Chester Hopewell

Silence interrupted by breezes rolling off distant waves, my lover and I carved messages into the undisturbed sands of this low-tide desert, our bodies sweeping aside the wrack washed ashore with yesterday's storm. Winged shadows flash across our darkening flesh as silver fins dot the horizon, we gaze upon the world unfolding before us, leaving the trappings of twisted society behind.

Josh Olenslager

DEC   82

Hey, it is great to hear from you! It's been much too long. I'm literally jotting this down as I run out the door. Life is busy, just get breakfast on the table and then it's midday or the day after and then back to work. I'm glad to hear that things have been going well. I miss the vein of creativity in old L-town. C'est la vie, enit?

Works Cited

Beowulf. (2000.) (S. Heaney, Trans.). New York, NY: W. W. Norton & Company.

Blom, I. "Frame, Space, Narrative. Doors, Windows and Mobile Framing in the Films of Luchino Visconti." *Acta Universitatis Sapientiae, Film and Media Studies. 2* (2010) 91-106. Retrieved from: http://www.acta.sapientia. ro/acta-film/C2/film2-5.pdf

Cruz, L. (2015). *Petite Hound Press: Issue 4.* Retrieved from http://www.petitehoundpress.com/#!issue-4/c9uy

Cruz, L. (2015). *Petite Hound Press: Issue 6.* Retrieved from http://www.petitehoundpress.com

Elderfield, J. (2008). Audio program excerpt MoMA audio: collection. Retrieved from https://www.moma.org/collection/browse_results.php?object_id=80538

Gale, Matthew. (2009). *Metaphysical art.* Retrieved from https://www.moma.org/collection/details.php?theme_id=10883

Larson, K. (2011). "The Oranges In Uganda." *Radial symmetry.* New Haven, Connecticut: Yale University Press.

Schirokauer, Conrad & Brown, Miranda. (2006). *A brief history of Chinese civilization* (2nd ed.). Belmont, CA: Thomson Higher Education.

Schulman, P. & Weinstein, J. A. (2015). Editors' Note. *Green Humanities*, 1, 1. Retrieved from http://greenhumanities.org/archives/vol1

Schulman, P. & Weinstein, J. A. (2015). *Green Humanities.* Retrieved from http://greenhumanities.org/archives/vol1

Young, G. & Buckley, C. (2012). *One for the money: the sentence as a poetic form.* Spokane, Washington: Lynx House Press.

The image in Naomi Ward's postcard:
Gulf of Alaska Seamount Expedition. Large paragorgia coral with galatheid crabs in a sponge forest on Welker Seamount at about 700 meters depth. Pacific Ocean, Gulf of Alaska.
(Public domain: By Gulf of Alaska 2004. NOAA Office of Ocean Exploration)

About the Correspondents

These days, **Heather Lang** reads and writes in coffee shops, on commuter ferries, and at a vegan punk rock bar in the Pacific Northwest.

H. L. Hix writes in one of his favorite indoor places, a former barn that he and his partner have renovated into a studio.

Kelli Russell Agodon is the author of six books, the cofounder of Two Sylvias Press and the Co-Director of Poets on the Coast. She lives in a sleepy seaside town near Seattle and has a fondness for typewriters, fedoras, and dessert. www.agodon.com / www.twosylviaspress.co

Kahle Alford can be found writing poetry in the wee hours of the morning somewhere between NYC and Nashville with her husband and their sweet, stinky dog.

Renée Ashley's most recent book, prose poems, is *Because I Am the Shore I Want to Be the Sea* (Subito Book Prize). She teaches in the MFA Program in Creative Writing at Fairleigh Dickinson University. *The View from the Body*, poems, will be published by Black Lawrence Press in 2016.

Pamela Banting lives under the spell of the natural grass prairie in the foothills of the Rocky Mountains west of Calgary, Alberta. She can see the mountains from her study. She can also see a fracking operation and a gas processing plant.

Anna Lena Phillips Bell writes, teaches, and edits in North Carolina. Her recent work includes *A Pocket Book of Forms*, a travel-sized guide to poetic forms. She can be reached at PO Box 713, Durham, NC 27702.

Lori Berezovsky lives in the middle of Kansas with her husband, two cats, and 29 fruit trees.

Edith "Ish" Bicknell is happiest near the ocean, in particular, the Penobscot Bay region of Maine. Her special loves are her daughter Adrien, music, and her girlfriend Rosemary. She is currently working for a major publisher on a digital online music education program.

Jeff Bloedel now lives and thrives in the Midwest with his three boys, two cats, and wonderful girlfriend.

Elizabeth Boleman-Herring is book-touring for her latest novel, which is set on Santorini, *The Visitors' Book (or Silva Rerum): An Erotic Fable*.

Nowadays, **Daniella Bondar** writes humor essays from her dollhouse-sized studio in Alphabet City. Occasionally with her one window open to fill the room with familiar sounds of car horns and intoxicated pedestrian fighting.

Alex Borgen is a true wanderer, off-road bicyclist, and interdisciplinary artist who always has a notebook and pen with her. She has since left Chicago in search of home.

A recent graduate of the MFA program at FDU, **Brian Bradford**'s first novel, *Greetings From Gravipause*, will be released by Jaded Ibis Press this December. He currently lives in New Jersey with his wife, Sadako, daughter Erin, two cavapoo, and an empty birdcage.

Di Brandt is the award-winning author of numerous books of poetry, fiction, creative essays, and literary criticism. Her latest poetry collection is *Walking to Mojácar*, with French and Spanish translations by Charles Leblanc and Ari Belathar. She lives in Canada.

Carol Fragale Brill, author of the novels, *Peace by Piece* and *Cape Maybe*, is a happily married beach and book lover who often finds inspiration for her writing on the Victorian streets and sandy beaches of Cape May A.K.A. Cape Amazing.

Beth Browne has been widely published both online and in print. In addition to writing and photographing, Browne manages a large farm and homeschools her two teenagers. Most weekends, she sails the North Carolina coast with her sweetie, Eric. For more information visit http://bethbrownebooks.com/

Choa Choi likes to write from the open terrace of Jennie's Cafe in Seoul in the mornings or at home while goofing around with an exercise ball.

Jan Conn writes as often as possible on a boat on the Amazon.

Alanna Coogan is a student at Marist College who loves to travel and study abroad.

Julianne Couch writes from the second story of her 1880 Victorian home in Bellevue, Iowa, overlooking the always opinionated Mississippi River.

Letisia Cruz writes and draws at her cat's favorite hangout — a small table directly beneath her kitchen window.

Dede Cummings writes from her off-the-grid home Vermont, but her soul belongs to her home state of Rhode Island where her creative nonfiction, *Spin Cycle*, is set.

Christine Cutler is a writer, editor, photographer, and guide. Anytime she can swing it, she travels to Italy to find peace and inspiration.

Renée E. D'Aoust divides her time between northern Idaho and southern Switzerland. Whether writing or hiking, her muse Tootsie is always by her side.

Gail Denham hails from Oregon.

Sophia Egbelo enjoys journeying where adventure takes her, with the goal to capture, write, and tell stories about the people, places, and cultures she has visited.

Melissa Esposito enjoys her writing time wherever she finds inspiration: sometimes a coffee shop, sometimes her bed, and sometimes sitting outside her horse's stall.

C. Lee Faris writes, photographs, and has other adventures mainly from the Pineywoods of East Texas. She tries to escape to mountains or coast as much as possible. You can find her on
Twitter: @travel_write
Instagram: @safe_travels
www.routineadventures.com

Arwen Fleming grew up on the road, spending time in Hardin County, Kentucky, Prince Edward Island, the Ottawa River Valley, and Edmonton, Alberta. She now lives in Montréal, where she is a graduate student in the Department of Communication Studies at Concordia University.

David Freitag has been a software programmer for a long time, but he has always tried to spend enough time outside to give himself a break from the technology that has threatened to consume his life.

Ron Frost is a geologist, a Buddhist, and the author of the book *Religion versus Science.*

Annie Guzzo is a composer who finds aural inspiration in prairies as well as metro stations.

Barbara Harroun is deeply rooted in Macomb, IL where she teaches and joyfully mothers her best creative endeavors, Annaleigh and Jack. When she isn't teaching, she can be found writing, reading, walking her beloved dog, Banjo, engaging in literacy activism, and practicing radical optimism.

A lifelong Alaskan, **Amy Hartley** writes poetry, enjoys exploring the outdoors with her family and hosts a jazz show on public radio. She lives in Fox, Alaska with her husband and two small kids.

Rick Hasenauer is retired and volunteers with a multi-arts organization (www.svanarts.org). **Patricia A. Nugent** is an author (*They Live On : Saying Goodbye to Mom and Dad*). Her upcoming manuscript, *Healing with Dolly Lama*, presents lessons learned from her golden retriever. The photograph of our dock on the Great Sacandaga Lake in the Adirondack Mountains of New York State was taken by Rick's brother, Jim Hasenauer.

April Heaney is a writer, teacher, and mother of three charmingly quirky children. She and her family travel to Ethiopia every few years to visit friends and family and soak up the beauty.

The great-granddaughter of pioneer ranchers, **Rachel Herbert** has returned to her roots and the family ranch near Nanton. At historic Trail's End she raises old-fashioned grassfed beef and chases her two free-range kids. When she's not feeding cows, or kids, she can be found reading, writing, riding, or with her hands in the dirt. Like the early ranching women featured in her 2011 University of Calgary Master's thesis, she knows a little bit about multi-tasking to keep the family ranch together.

Duane L. Herrmann is a survivor who lived and was farming on a tractor by age 13. His continued connection to the land is reflected in his stories and poems. He is now a historian of the Bahai Faith in Kansas with work published in the US and other places.

William D. Hicks is a writer/artist who lives in Chicago, Illinois by himself. Any offers? He is not related to the famous comedian Bill Hicks, though he's just as funny in his own right. His poetry, fiction, art, and photography appear in numerous magazines. Visit https://www.flickr.com/photos/50227262@N07/ to see more of his art/photos.

If you can't find **Fran Hill** on the little porch, she might be found at the local community making props.

Chester Hopewell brings poetry to the streets, posting his original poems on telephone poles for people to encounter in their everyday lives.

A New Yorker by birth, **Christina Ingoglia** teaches writing in Columbia, Missouri, a place she hadn't heard of until 2009.

Cory Johnston does most of his writing in small New Jersey towns, his view of the Emerald Isle blocked by the distance and the waves.

Kevin Keen has a day job, but his passion is photography. He lives in Geneva, Switzerland.

Charity Kittler and her camera enjoy exploring cities together, and now make their home in New York City.

Jeff Knops recently moved to Seattle and has a hard time not taking a picture every 12'.

Brenda Kay Ledford is a native of Clay County, North Carolina. She's a retired educator, and a professional writer. She's a member of North Carolina Writer's Network, and listed with a Directory of American Poets and Fiction Writers. Finishing Line Press published her three poetry books that received the Paul Green Award from the North Carolina Society of Historians. Aldrich Press published her latest book *Crepe Roses*.

Tracey Michae'l Lewis-Giggetts often has to go away to write in order to find her story; as far away as a hotel room on some random shore or mining the cavernous parts of her mind while sitting on the front porch.

Timothy Lindner reads on the train to and from work and writes on nights and weekends at his suburban apartment.

Jeff Lockwood writes on an aging computer at a manufactured desk (sometimes at the dining room table). He really wants to write with an elegant pen in a funky notebook under a shady tree, but he lacks the self-discipline.

Danielle Lorenz is a PhD student in the Department of Educational Policy Studies at the University of Alberta whose work examines settler colonialism in education. She also endeavours to befriend the white-tailed jackrabbits of amiskwaciwâskahikan/pêhonan/Treaty Six/Edmonton (so far it is not going so well).

Rupert Loydell is a notebook carrier, who writes wherever he is. His favourite places include Italy, London, and Manhattan.

John C. Mannone has over 400 works in *Artemis*, *Still*, *Town Creek Poetry*, *The Baltimore Review*, and others. He's poetry editor for *Silver Blade* and *Abyss & Apex*, won the 2015 Joy Margrave Award for creative nonfiction and nominated three times for the Pushcart. Visit The Art of Poetry: http://jcmannone.wordpress.com

John Manuel reports: I am an Ohio native who moved to North Carolina in the 1970s. I have authored a guidebook, *The Natural Traveler Along North Carolina's Coast*, and a memoir, *The Canoeist*, about my coming of age on the rivers of the eastern U.S. I have traveled all over the world, but one of my favorite spots remains the shale ravines of Northeast Ohio.

Kaitlin McClary, cat-lover and yogurt enthusiast, is currently working toward her MFA in the Writing for Children program at The New School.

Erik Molvar is a Wyoming conservationist who has been exploring the Red Desert for two decades.

Stephen Mulkey and **Michele Leavitt** live in Maine most of the time, where Stephen serves as President of Unity College, Michele teaches writing, and their two dogs run the show.

Tendai R. Mwanaka is a multidisciplinary artist from Chitungwiza, Zimbabwe. His works with essays, non-fictions, poetry, plays, fictions, music, sound art, photography, drawings, paintings, video, collage, mixed medias, inter-genres, and inter-disciplines…

A former ballet dancer whose career was cut short by the onset of rheumatoid arthritis and author of the poetry collection *Roundabout Directions to Lincoln Center* (Urban Farmhouse Press 2014), **Renée K. Nicholson** splits her artistic pursuits between writing and dance.

Josh Olenslager still makes a wish each night before sleeping.

Emilene Ostlind puts her creative nonfiction MFA to work wrestling with western natural resource conundrums as a storyteller and editor for *Western Confluence* magazine at the University of Wyoming.

A native New Yorker, **James Penha** <jamespenha.com> has lived for the past quarter-century in Indonesia.

J.C. Pérez-Duthie loves to teach, write, and travel. Not a bad way to make a living.

No longer living in her truck in the Wyoming desert, **Shelby Perry** now spends her days rambling through the wilds of Vermont where she is a masters student in the UVM Field Naturalist program.

Bernard Quetchenbach lives in Billings, Montana, and teaches at Montana State University Billings. His latest book is *The Hermit's Place*, a poetry collection from Wild Leaf Press.

Bill Reiners, now retired, no longer does field research and spends much of his time in the Sonoran desert, far from foggy forests.

Richard Retzlaff is a tattooed, canoe-paddling, bike-riding ceramicist who lives near Madison, WI.

Jean-Paul Richard reports: I enjoy spending more time in the outdoors now that I have reached the age where I can take life at a slower pace. I still enjoy writing about the outdoors however, when stuck indoors, and encourage that avocation by belonging to the Hampton Roads Writers Group.

Suzanne Richter is an avid neighborhood walker and freelance writer currently living in Nashville, TN. Some of her favorite things are coffee, puppy hugs, blue jeans, and colored glass.

When she is not at Black Rock City, **Suzanne Roberts** writes and teaches in South Lake Tahoe, California.

Tazio Ruffilo lives in the always busy Paterson, New Jersey, but likes to get as far away from the city as possible to do his work, usually a coffee shop in the Hudson Valley.

Under a skyfull of permanent stars, **Anna Sangrey** seeks wonder in her first love, the woods and fields of Pennsylvania, while writing towards imagination and the community she calls home.

Brenda Saunders is a Sydney poet and artist. She has written three collections of poetry, her latest *the sound of red* (Gindinderra Press 2013) features poems inspired by art and travel. As a bird watcher Brenda enjoys travelling in Australia's wild places. Her next book will feature poems about our unique Australian environment.

Leah Schultz and her husband spend most of their spare time caring for their four children, all of whom are quadrupeds. During the day, Leah can be found working in the ugliest building on the University of Wisconsin campus. Her nights are typically spent making music, sipping Wisconsin microbrews, or binge watching television shows on Netflix.

Ed Sherline has not made as many trips to the dump since they started charging by the pound, but they have cheap compost.

Sally Showalter's main writing space is in her studio that looks into a garden with her two cats sitting on the window sill.

tom (WordWulf) sterner wrestles with creativity: graphic art, music, photography, & WORD. A native Coloradoan, he lives in Denver. Tom's artwork, music, photography, & written word have been published in magazines & on the internet, including *Howling Dog Press/Omega, Carpe Articulum Literary Review, Skyline Literary Review, Storyteller,* & *Flashquake*. http://wordwulf.com

Dan Stockman is a veteran newspaper journalist who now has a day job writing about Catholic nuns. In his spare time he writes and teaches writing, runs, and learns martial arts with his children in Indiana.

Emily Strauss often travels alone through the West, with camera and notebook, the notebook being the primary tool for her poetry. She rises early, sleeps early, hikes, writes, reads, and watches birds. She has over 250 poems published in many US and foreign venues, and some photos also.

Stefan Strychar is engaged in a long, ongoing tug-of-war over whether he should focus on being a poet or a musician, and has yet to figure out that they are not mutually exclusive.

In her home studio and community groups, **Linda Aleta Tame** expresses her spiritual quest through writing, visual art and conversation.

Tynia Thomassie is in her favorite place almost every day, which, then allows her to be present to any other place, state, or situation that presents itself thereafter.

Jenna Tripke lives in Philadelphia, where she works a 9-5 and files her taxes every year by February 1st. Her favorite colors are beige and light beige.

Naomi Ward now studies microbes that live within the human body, rather than the deep ocean, which is rather inaccessible from a high plain in southeast Wyoming.

Josh A. Weinstein teaches English and environmental studies at Virginia Wesleyan College, nestled in the Chesapeake Bay watershed, where he lives with his family. He recently co-founded the new online journal *Green Humanities* <greenhumanities.org>.

Paula Wright continues to write from Eugene, Oregon.

Randolyn Zinn is a writer and director who spent time in Spain thanks to a Jerome Foundation travel grant.